General E

GW00866551

DEATH CAMP
ON THE RIVER KWAI

THE STORY OF ERNEST GORDON

Roger J. Owen

THE RELIGIOUS EDUCATION PRESS
A Division of Pergamon Press

The Religious Education Press
A Division of Pergamon Press
Hennock Road, Exeter EX2 8RP

Pergamon Press Ltd
Headington Hill Hall, Oxford OX3 0BW

Pergamon Press Inc.
Maxwell House, Fairview Park, Elmsford, New York 10523

Pergamon Press Canada Ltd
Suite 104, 150 Consumers Road, Willowdale, Ontario M2J 1P9

Pergamon Press (Australia) Pty Ltd
P.O. Box 544, Potts Point, N.S.W. 2011

Pergamon Press GmbH
Hammerweg 6, D-6242 Kronberg, Federal Republic of Germany

Photographs are reproduced by courtesy of The Revd Dr Ernest
Gordon (pp. 3, 24) and the Imperial War Museum (pp. 2, 9, 14, 21).
Drawings (pp. 12, 18) are reproduced by courtesy of Ronald Searle.
Cover illustration by Gary Long.

First published 1981

Reprinted 1982

Printed in Great Britain by A. Wheaton & Co. Ltd, Exeter

ISBN 0 08-025642-2 non net
ISBN 0 08-025643-0 net

DEATH CAMP ON THE RIVER KWAI

The Story of Ernest Gordon

In the Second World War, Japanese prisoner-of-war camps were terrible places to be in. Prisoners were murdered by being beaten, stabbed, drowned or even beheaded. Others were killed more slowly, by being made to work until they dropped dead from exhaustion or lack of food. Many were slowly tortured to death. Others died simply because they were given no medical care when they fell ill.

Prisoners who disobeyed orders were treated very harshly. Some had their hands crushed in vices. Others were forced to drink a lot of water, and then were jumped on. Others were hung from trees by their thumbs.

A British officer called Ernest Gordon was put in one of the worst of these camps.

At war

Ernest was born and brought up in Scotland. When he left school, he started to train as an R.A.F. pilot, but when he broke his spine and his skull in a plane crash his training came to a sudden end. Fortunately, he recovered from his injuries.

Ernest decided to go to university. But in 1939, war broke out, and he had to abandon his studies.

He joined up to fight for his country, and became an officer in a battalion of the Argyll and Sutherland Highlanders, one of the most famous regiments in the British Army.

Ernest spent the first few months of the war in training. Then he was sent to France for a while, where he saw action against the enemy for the first time. After this he was sent to Malaya. He travelled down across the Red Sea and the Indian Ocean on a troop-ship, moving further and further away from his home in Scotland. The next part of the journey took him through the hot, steamy jungles of Malaya, travelling on foot.

Argyll and Sutherland Highlanders wading across a river in Malaya

On 8 December 1941, Japanese forces invaded northern Malaya. The soldiers were the best in the Japanese Army and were skilled jungle fighters. The British soldiers, on the other hand, had not been properly trained for jungle warfare. The Japanese quickly forced the British troops to retreat.

After only fifty-four days' fighting, the whole of Malaya was in the hands of the Japanese. There had been a thousand men in Ernest's battalion when it left Scotland. Now only 120 were left. Another ninety were killed trying to defend the island of Singapore, at the tip of Malaya. After sixteen days, the island fell.

Ernest and some others found a boat and crossed the sea to the island of Sumatra. Here Ernest made his way to the coastal town of Padang.

The last British warship had sailed from Padang a few days before Ernest got there. What was he to do? Sumatra

Ernest Gordon (right foreground) in Malaya

was about to be taken over by the Japanese, and the enemy was already closing in on Padang.

As he was walking down the main street, Ernest bumped into an army officer he knew, a colonel. The colonel led the way to a café which had a few iron tables out on the street. A waiter brought them coffee. When the waiter had moved away, the colonel looked hard at Ernest.

"It's very unlikely that any help is going to get through to us before the Japanese take over. I'm forming an escape party. Would you like to join us?"

"Of course I would!" exclaimed Ernest. "What's the plan?"

The colonel leaned closer across the table. "I've got hold of two cars to travel overland. I'm told there's a chance we may be able to buy a sailing-boat at a fishing village called Sasok, about a hundred miles north of here."

"Yes, that sounds possible," agreed Ernest. "We can sail for Ceylon. It can't be more than twelve hundred miles away."

The colonel frowned. "But it won't be all that easy. The Japanese Navy and Air Force are all over the Indian Ocean."

"How many of us are going?" asked Ernest.

"Ten. But it'll be a risky business. If we're caught we'll almost certainly be killed."

On the run

So at five o'clock in the morning the ten men left Padang by car. Soon they came across signs of the Japanese. They crossed a bridge. A few minutes later they heard a muffled *boom*. The bridge had been blown up! Later, they turned off the main road on to a single-track road that wound and twisted up into the hills. From the top of the first rise they saw the dust of marching Japanese soldiers rising from the road they had just left.

It took nearly twelve hours to reach Sasok. They bought a boat from some local Malay people. The boat was about fifteen metres long and rather broad. Its deck-house ran almost the length of the boat, leaving only a short deck space at both ends.

The following day was spent buying and loading food on to the boat and checking the rigging and ropes. Oil drums and petrol cans were filled with water. In all they collected nearly 3000 litres! That was enough for at least thirty days. They had two baskets of tinned food, two sacks of rice and plenty of fruit.

In the evening twilight the boat left Sasok. At first all went well. They even sighted a Japanese gunboat, but managed to get their boat into a creek surrounded by trees, so that they were not seen. Every day they travelled 50 to 60 kilometres closer to Ceylon and safety.

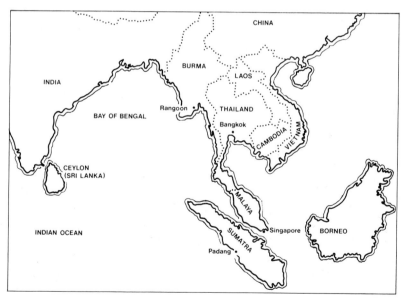

Then fever struck. One by one the men fell ill from malaria, a fever caused by the bite of the mosquito. They all recovered in the end, but while anyone was ill there were fewer men to do the work on the boat. Also everyone was weaker.

They were well over half-way to Ceylon when the look-out shouted out, "Smoke ahoy!"

Soon everyone was on deck, straining their eyes to see what was on the horizon.

"There are three ships!" someone exclaimed.

"Yes, I can see the funnels," added Ernest.

"Shall we signal to them?" asked another.

"No! No!" answered the senior officer. "They might be the enemy."

One of the men dressed up in some Chinese coolie's clothes which they had brought with them – a wide cone-shaped straw hat and a long jacket. They hoped he would look like a local fisherman to the Japanese. He sat by the tiller and steered the boat. The rest went out of sight below.

The ships came nearer. At last the man at the tiller shouted out, "They look like tankers. . . . Yes, they are tankers."

"Are they the enemy?" asked the senior officer.

"Can't tell yet. But they must be. Ours wouldn't be in these waters."

"Where are they now?"

"They're still coming in our direction."

The hidden men held their breath.

"Still coming . . . still coming . . . still coming . . . they're about a mile off . . . they're the enemy, all right . . . they're drawing away from us . . . still drawing away . . . still drawing away . . . they're well past us. . . . Oh, no! One of them is turning."

There was a flash from a gun on the tanker's deck,

followed by the sharp crack of the explosion. Then there was a *whoosh* overhead and a shell fell fifty metres from the boat.

The tanker came close. Its rails were lined with sailors – Japanese sailors. A rope-ladder was thrown over the side of the tanker and the men were ordered to climb aboard. The sailors grabbed Ernest roughly. They twisted his arms behind his back. He was searched and then forced to stand with the muzzle of a pistol pressed tightly against the side of his head.

One of the Japanese officers came up. "You will all be questioned one at a time," he said in broken English, "and then you will be shot. You are spies!"

All day they were questioned, one by one. Late in the day the senior officer was questioned again. He came back looking a little less worried.

"It's all right," he told Ernest and the others. "They've changed their minds. They're not going to shoot us after all. We're to be treated as prisoners of war and taken back to Singapore for further questioning."

Four days later they arrived at the docks of Singapore and were taken to the prison camp at Changi, about twenty kilometres away. So began Ernest Gordon's three and a half years as a prisoner of war in Japanese prison camps.

Changi Camp

There were 40 000 prisoners at Changi, but only enough huts for a thousand of them to sleep under cover at night. Some of the prisoners were taken to form work parties. They had to clean up the nearby city or load up Japanese ships in the Singapore docks. Working at the docks was a job the prisoners liked because it gave them a chance to buy or steal food.

Ernest had not been long in Changi when he was chosen to lead a work party at the docks. An officer from another unit came up to Ernest.

"Could you do me a favour?"

"What is it?" asked Ernest.

"Well, I've a friend dying of beriberi," replied the officer. (Beriberi is a disease which people get from not eating food with enough vitamins in it.) "If you could get hold of a jar of Marmite," the officer went on, "it might save his life. Marmite's got a lot of vitamin B in it."

While half of Ernest's work party loaded the ship, the other half raided the dockside warehouses. Some of the men distracted the Japanese guards by staging fights and arguments.

Ernest went into one warehouse and to his surprise quickly found a jar of Marmite. He tucked it under his shirt and returned to the dockside. This was the first time he had ever stolen anything, but he did not feel it was wrong. After all, he was doing it to save someone's life.

A few days later Ernest suffered a violent attack of fever. It was malaria again. He had scarcely recovered when the camp doctor discovered that Ernest had worms. (In hot countries you can easily swallow worms' eggs if you eat dirty food or drink dirty water. The worms hatch out inside your body and make you ill.)

Having got rid of the worms, the doctor found that Ernest needed to have his appendix taken out. They laid him out on a kitchen table and placed a pad with a few drops of ether on it over his mouth. He quickly lost consciousness. Although the operation was not done in a proper hospital, it was successful.

Then Ernest and some of the other prisoners were moved

to a camp in Thailand, at a place called Banpong. Conditions here were even worse than those at Changi Camp. There was no bedding, the food was still poor, and the guards were more violent. The work was very hard. Every day the prisoners were sent out to clear ground in the jungle.

A few months later they were marched to another camp, further north again. It was at Chungkai, on the bank of the River Kwai. When they arrived, Ernest and the other prisoners were not allowed to rest for long. They were split up into work parties almost straight away and told to build their own huts.

The walls of the huts were made of bamboo. The roofs were made of palm leaves. Inside there were sleeping-platforms made of split bamboo rising just above the mud. Each man had to himself an area about two metres long and half a metre wide—roughly the size of a narrow grave.

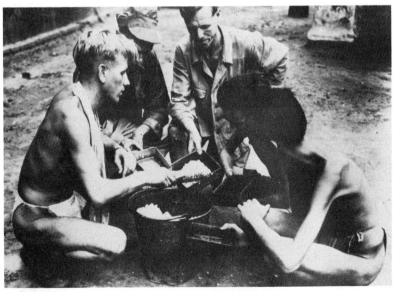

Sharing out a meal of rice, the prisoners' staple food

The railway

The prisoners at Chungkai were to be used to build a railway for the Japanese Army. The Japanese were planning to go through Burma and invade India, and they wanted to build a railway through Thailand linking up with the Burma Railway, which ran from China to India.

This new railway, known as the Kwai Railway, would have to cut through hundreds of kilometres of jungle and hills. The Japanese wanted it finished in twelve months! In October 1942 work began on the railway.

Every morning at dawn the prisoners were marched out of Chungkai to work. They were marched back again late at night. This went on for seven days a week, without rest-days or holidays. Of course, it was quite wrong for any country to treat its prisoners of war like this.

Towards the spring of 1943, the Japanese guards grew more and more worried that the railway would not be finished on time. They stood over the prisoners with thick bamboo sticks, yelling "Speedo! Speedo!" If the prisoners did not move fast enough, the guards beat them savagely. Many of the prisoners no longer had the strength to bear such beatings. They fell to the ground and died. But human life was cheap. The guards simply did not care.

Escape was impossible. Hundreds of kilometres of jungle surrounded the camp. A few prisoners tried to get away, but none survived.

Death was everywhere. Once a guard flew into a rage and hurled a hammer at a prisoner's head. A Japanese engineer ordered two prisoners to prepare a dynamite charge and, while they were still carrying out his instructions, he set off the charge and blew them to pieces. Once a boulder was pushed off a ledge, crushing a group of

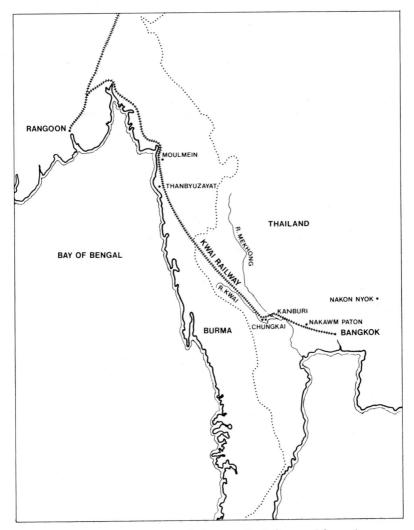

prisoners below. Other prisoners died from thirst, hunger, exhaustion and disease.

Things were getting so bad that the prisoners themselves were becoming more selfish. Many of them stole from each other – usually food or a blanket. Some even robbed the dead, taking a ring, a pen, or even the rags they wore.

11

Fit parade for work on the Kwai Railway (drawn by Ronald Searle, 1943)

The Death House

The camp hospital was known as the Death House. Ernest had to go there when he caught a disease called diphtheria. The floor of the hospital was a sea of mud. The smell was terrible: sickness, overflowing toilets, unwashed and even rotting bodies. Flies swarmed about them by day, and bedbugs crawled over them by night.

All the hospital staff were British prisoners. The "nurses" were called orderlies; they were just ordinary soldiers with a little medical training. There were a few medical officers who were doctors.

"Get me out of here!" begged Ernest to a passing orderly, after spending several days in the hospital.

"Can't," said the orderly with a shrug.

"Why not?" asked Ernest.

"Nowhere else for you to go," replied the orderly.

"How about letting me lie at the entrance? It's cleaner there and I'd get some fresh air."

"Can't. You'd be in our way."

"How about the far end, then?"

"That's where we put the dead bodies."

"It's cleaner over there than it is here, isn't it?"

"Yes."

"Then please move me!" pleaded Ernest.

"O.K. then. If that's how you want it. But mind, if anyone puts a sack on you while you're asleep, you'd better make a noise or move or something. We wouldn't want to bury you alive!"

That night Ernest's companions were ten dead men wrapped in rice-sacks.

Ernest was now very ill. One evening one of his friends came to see him in the Death House. He told Ernest that he had got some friends to build a tiny hut specially for him. The Japanese thought Ernest was dying, so they did not mind. All that was needed was permission from one of the British doctors for him to be moved.

When the medical officer was making his morning rounds, Ernest whispered to him, "How about letting me out of this hole? Some friends have built a hut for me. There's not much more you can do for me, is there?"

"No, Ernie, there isn't" replied the medical officer. "I only wish there were. I'll ask the chief medical officer."

An hour later, the medical officer returned with the

British prisoners in the prison camp at Rangoon

chief medical officer. They stood away from Ernest, thinking that he could not hear them.

"What's his present condition?" asked the chief doctor.

"His blood count is bad. And his pulse is very weak."

"The only thing left is to let him have a decent end. He can't walk, can he?"

"No, he can't. But I'm sure his friends will help him. It won't be for long, in any case."

So they moved him out of the hospital into the hut, thinking he would soon die.

Brave actions

But Ernest gradually got better, mainly because of two men who looked after him. They took it in turns to wash him, talk to him and bring him food. Remarkably, after a few weeks Ernest was able to walk with the help of a stick.

One of these men had been at school with Ernest. His

name was Dennis Moore, but he was usually called by his nickname, Dinty. The other man was a stranger who had come to Ernest's hut to offer him help. His name was Dusty Miller.

Dinty was full of fun and had a great love of life. He was a Roman Catholic. Dusty was a calm, quiet, gentle man. He was a Methodist. In their different ways, both men had a deep Christian faith.

Dinty and Dusty were not the only ones who helped their fellow-prisoners. At first all the men were suffering so much that most of them could only think about themselves. But lately more and more of them had begun to help each other. They had become less wrapped up in their own problems and had started to think more about the needs of others. This happened because they were encouraged by the brave or kind actions of several of the prisoners.

For example, there was one soldier called Angus, a big, strong fellow. His best friend was ill and his blanket had been stolen, so Angus gave him his own blanket. He also slipped out of the camp at night to visit nearby villages and buy food for his friend. His friend recovered, but Angus died of hunger and exhaustion.

Another man showed great courage at the end of work one day. When the prisoners' tools were collected up, the Japanese guard insisted that one of the shovels was missing. He lost his temper and demanded that the man who had taken the shovel should step forward. Nobody moved. In a rage, the guard screamed, "All die! All die!"

The guard aimed his rifle at one of the prisoners, and was about to fire, when another prisoner stepped forward and said calmly, "I did it." Seizing his rifle by the barrel, the guard lifted it high in the air and brought it down on the prisoner's head. The man sank to the ground, dead. When the tools were counted again, all the shovels were

15

there. The guard had made a mistake when he counted them the first time.

One example of kindness shown by the local villagers occurred at about the same time. When they were marched through the villages on their way to work, the prisoners were usually sneered at. People often held their noses as the prisoners went by, to suggest that they were smelly. But one day the prisoners went through a village where the people gave them cakes, bananas and eggs, and even pushed money into their hands.

The prisoners later discovered that these villagers had once been Buddhists, but had been converted to Christianity by missionaries. (Buddhism is the main religion in Thailand.) Ernest began to wonder whether there was more to Christianity than he had thought.

One evening, feeling rather miserable, he said to Dusty, "Sometimes it's hard to see any point in living."

"I see a lot of point in living," replied Dusty.

"But we begin to die as soon as we're born," Ernest continued.

"There's more to life than that," answered his friend. "I don't think it's an accident that we are born. God has a purpose for us."

"Do you really believe that?" asked Ernest, for he had never bothered much about God.

"Yes, I do!"

"Then why doesn't He do something, instead of just sitting on His great big white throne in heaven?" asked Ernest.

Dusty thought for a moment. "We can't see everything He's doing now. I suppose one day we'll see and then we'll understand."

Dusty had a Bible. He opened it and read aloud: "There is no fear in love. But perfect love drives out fear.... If

16

anyone says 'I love God', yet hates his brother, he is a liar. For anyone who does not love his brother, whom he has seen, cannot love God, whom he has not seen."

Ernest thought about these words. Both Dusty and Dinty showed that there was some truth in them, by the way they helped him. Perhaps there was a God, after all, he thought.

Faith in God

Then some of the prisoners asked Ernest to lead a discussion group about the Christian faith. This made him study the New Testament. He had a Bible but had not bothered to read it. It had been given to him by a soldier who wanted to lighten his pack before being marched to another camp.

Through reading the New Testament, Ernest came to believe that Jesus was a real person. He realised that the love seen in the life of Jesus was God's love. It was a love that really cared about people's suffering. This made it easier for him to believe in God. The death of Jesus on the Cross showed that God, through Jesus, knew what suffering was. Ernest could not explain why people suffered as they did, but at least he understood that God cared.

Ernest was slowly becoming a Christian. This was not pie-in-the-sky religion. It was a living faith which was very practical. He was able to help the sick and dying in ways which he had never thought possible.

For example a teen-age soldier lay dying. Germs had got into his wounds and his flesh was rotting. Ernest visited him.

"I'm scared," admitted the lad. "I'm so scared at times that I can't think."

"What are you scared of ?" asked Ernest.

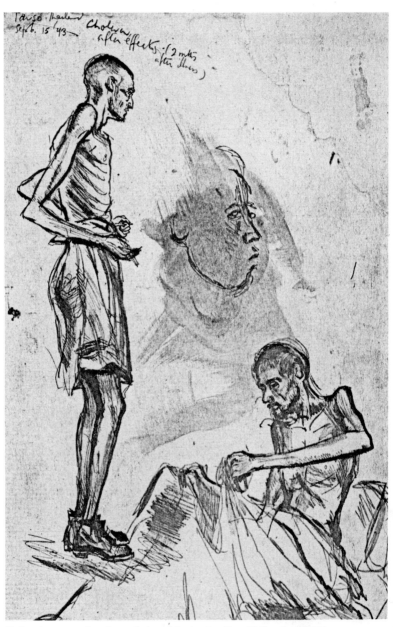

Prisoners recovering from cholera (drawn by Ronald Searle, 1943)

18

"All kinds of things. I'm scared of the Japs. I'm scared I'm going to die."

Ernest said the only thing he could think of. "We'll help you not to be scared. We'll stay by you."

"Thank you. That's good to know. I'm going to die, aren't I?"

Ernest cleared his throat, trying to find the right words. "That's something we all have to face. I've faced it – so have a lot of others."

"I know," the boy nodded. "You've been through it. You understand." Then he added. "My mother and dad will miss me. I'm the only one they've got and they'll be so lonely when I don't come back."

"Here, let me read you something that may help," offered Ernest.

Ernest opened his Bible and read from Psalm 23: "Even though I walk through the valley of the shadow of death, I will fear no evil, for You are with me." He flicked over the pages and came to some words of Jesus: "I am the resurrection and the life. He who believes in me will live, even though he dies. . . ."

The dying soldier found comfort in these words. "Everything's going to be all right," he murmured. Two days later, he died.

Gradually more and more of the prisoners began to believe in God. This gave them fresh hope and courage. They began to take more interest in life. They used their spare time for doing useful things. One group of men made simple artificial legs for the prisoners who had had their legs cut off. Another group made a garden, putting in it plants from the jungle. Those with special skills or knowledge began to teach others. A library, a drama group and an art and craft club were formed. From time to time the prisoners held singsongs.

An orchestra was started. Soon there were plenty of instruments. Some gift parcels arrived in the camp from the International Y.M.C.A. (Young Men's Christian Association). Among them were six violins. The prisoners themselves made drums and cymbals from oil barrels and animal skins from the camp slaughterhouse. Wind instruments were made by cutting holes in bamboo canes with a penknife.

They even built a church. It was really not much more than a clearing in the jungle, but it was a special place for prayer and worship. A cross and a lamp were placed on a table of bamboo. The cross was a carved piece of wood. The lamp was a tin can with a shoe-lace as a wick. A small roof of palm leaves protected the cross and the lamp from the weather.

Every evening a service was held at which prayers were said for the sick, for those at home in Britain and for the daily needs of the prisoners. Men prayed for strength to face the hardships that lay ahead. They prayed for a peaceful night's sleep. They prayed about almost anything.

Yet it was not easy for Ernest and the others to say the Lord's Prayer: "And forgive us our trespasses [sins] as we forgive those who trespass [sin] against us." That meant forgiving the Japanese guards who were treating them so cruelly. It was not until Good Friday 1945 that Ernest felt able to forgive the enemy. On that day he remembered the words of Jesus on the cross: "Father, forgive them, for they do not know what they are doing."

Helping the enemy

The railway was completed in the autumn of 1943. The following spring, the camp at Chungkai began to be closed

A bridge on the Kwai Railway near Thanbyuzayat after an attack by R.A.F. bombers

down. The healthier prisoners were sent to work in Japan. The remaining thousands were sent in groups to other camps. It was autumn before Ernest was sent to join a camp in Nakawm Paton.

Nakawm Paton was a camp for those who were ill or recovering from illness. There were separate huts for men suffering from different illnesses: one for men with beriberi, another for men with leprosy, another for those who had gone mad, another for those suffering from dysentery, and so on.

At first everyone seemed filled with despair and gloom. However, by being helpful and cheerful, Ernest and some of his friends from Chungkai soon brought a new spirit into the camp. The change which had taken place at Chungkai took place at Nakawm Paton too.

Shortly after Easter 1945 Ernest was moved again. This time it was about 100 kilometres west to Kanburi, only a few kilometres from Chungkai! Then this whole camp was moved first by train and then on foot to Nakon Nyok, north-east of Bangkok.

On the way the prisoners were shunted on to a siding for a while. They found themselves alongside a train full of wounded Japanese soldiers. The soldiers were in a shocking state. Their uniforms were covered in blood and mud, and their wounds were full of pus and maggots. They were on their own without any medical care.

For the first time Ernest understood why the Japanese were so cruel to their prisoners. If they did not look after their own soldiers, why should they bother about their enemies?

Without a word, most of the prisoners around Ernest took out part of their rations. Then, with water-bottles and food in their hands, they went over to the Japanese soldiers to help them. Ernest and the others knelt beside their enemies. They gave them food and water, cleaned and bound up their wounds and said a few kind words to them. Grateful cries of "Aragatto!" ("Thank you!") followed them when they left.

A British officer from another section of the train came up to Ernest. "What fools you are!" he said. "Don't you realise that they are the enemy?"

"Have you never heard the story of the Good Samaritan?" asked Ernest.

The officer stared at him blankly, so Ernest went on. "A man was travelling from Jerusalem to Jericho. On the way he was attacked by thugs and left to die. Along came a priest. He passed him by. Then came a Levite, a worker in the Temple. He passed him by as well. Next came a despised Samaritan, an enemy. But he didn't pass by. He stopped. His heart was filled with pity. He knelt down and cleaned and dressed the helpless man's wounds. Then

22

he took him to an inn where he had him cared for at his own expense."

"But that's different!" the officer protested. "That's in the Bible." Pointing at the Japanese, he added, "These are the swine who've starved us and beaten us. They've murdered our friends. These are our enemies."

At that moment, Ernest remembered some other words that Jesus said: "Love your enemies and pray for those who persecute you."

Freedom

In August 1945 Ernest and his fellow-prisoners were set free. The Second World War was over. The Japanese, like the Germans, had finally surrendered.

Ernest wondered what had happened to some of his friends. He had not seen Dinty Moore or Dusty Miller since those days in Chungkai. Eventually he found out what had happened from people who brought Red Cross supplies and letters to the camp.

Dinty was killed on his way to a camp in Japan. He and the other prisoners were locked up in the ship's hold for the voyage. When the ship was torpedoed by an American submarine, there was no chance of escape for the men in the hold.

For a long time there was no word about Dusty. Then at last Ernest met someone who had been with Dusty cutting a road through the jungle for the Japanese in Burma.

"He hadn't done anything wrong. The Jap officer in charge hated him because he couldn't break him. You know how he was – a good man if ever there was one. That's why he hated him."

"So what did the Japs do to him?" asked Ernest.

"Strung him up on a tree. Crucified him."

Ernest Gordon as Dean of Princeton University, 1979

Tears clouded Ernest's eyes. There on a tree, like Jesus, Dusty had died. So far from his homeland, so far from everyone, yet so near to God.

Ernest returned to Scotland. It was six years since he had last been there. He was found to be suffering from, among other things, malaria, a swollen liver and an enlarged heart. He had to spend eight weeks in hospital.

When Ernest was better, he wondered what to do with the rest of his life. At first he thought of staying in the army, but as a Christian he wanted to help people. He decided that the best way of doing this was to become a church minister. After training, he became a minister in 1950.

He also had a strong desire to work among young people. A few years later he was able to combine the two when he was put in charge of the Chapel of Princeton University in the United States of America. He did this job until he retired in 1981.

What had Ernest learnt by his experiences in the prisoner-of-war camps? This is what he wrote in 1963: "I know something of suffering and what it means to look death in the face. I know the depths to which men can sink and the heights to which they can rise. I can speak from experience of despair, but also of hope; of hatred, but also of love; of man without God, but also of man helped by God."

Ernest Gordon not only lived through the Death Camp on the River Kwai. He also found the living God there, and has spent the rest of his life helping other people to find Him also.

BIOGRAPHICAL NOTES

Ernest Gordon was born in Greenock in Scotland on 31 May 1916. He trained as a pilot with the R.A.F. before studying history and philosophy at the University of Glasgow.

In 1939 he was posted to one of the battalions of the Argyll and Sutherland Highlanders – the 93rd Highlanders – as a second lieutenant. In March 1941 he was promoted to captain and became a company commander. He was captured by the Japanese in 1942 and spent three and a half years in a succession of prisoner-of-war camps.

From January 1946 to June 1947 Ernest attended the Scottish Congregational College in Edinburgh; from 1948 to 1950 he did post-graduate studies at Hartford Theological Seminary in Connecticut, U.S.A.

In 1950 Ernest was ordained a Church of Scotland minister and was assistant minister at the Abbey of Paisley in Scotland from 1950 to 1953. He then spent a year supplying the pulpit at two Presbyterian churches on Long Island, New York. In 1954 he became Presbyterian chaplain at Princeton University, New Jersey. In the following year he was appointed Dean of the Chapel of Princeton University. He retired as Dean in July 1981. He is now president of Creed, an organisation seeking to help those who are imprisoned for their beliefs.

Ernest Gordon has several degrees, including doctorates in divinity and literature. In 1963 his book *Miracle on the River Kwai* was published and became a best seller.

THINGS TO DO

A Test yourself

Here are some short questions. See if you can remember the answers from what you have read. Then write them down in a few words.

1 Why did Ernest Gordon's training as a pilot suddenly come to an end?
2 How is malaria caused?
3 Why did Ernest steal some Marmite?
4 How soon did the Japanese want the railway finished?
5 What was the hospital at Chungkai Camp called?
6 What is the main religion in Thailand?
7 Which part of the Lord's Prayer did the prisoners find difficult to say?
8 Which Bible story did Ernest tell the officer who thought it was foolish to help the wounded Japanese soldiers?
9 How did Dinty die?
10 What job did Ernest train for after the war?

B Think through

These questions need longer answers. Think about them, and try to write two or three sentences in answer to each one. You may look up the story again to help you.

1 Why did the Japanese want a railway built through Thailand?
2 What was the main reason why Ernest got better after he had been so ill that the doctors thought he would die?
3 Why were the villagers in one village kinder to the prisoners than those in other villages?
4 How did Dusty and Dinty help Ernest to believe in God?
5 How did Ernest come to believe that Jesus was a real person?
6 How did Ernest help the young soldier who was dying?
7 In what ways did Chungkai Camp improve when the prisoners had more faith?

C Talk about

Here are some questions for you to discuss together. Try to

give reasons for what you say or think. Try to find out all the different opinions which people have about each question.

1 When, if ever, is it right to steal? Was Ernest right to steal the Marmite?
2 Why did things get better at Chungkai Camp?
3 What gave the prisoner the courage to say he had taken a shovel, when he knew the guard would beat or kill him?
4 Why are people sometimes cruel to one another?
5 Is it right for Christian missionaries to tell people of other religions about Christ?
6 Why does God allow suffering? How does the death of Jesus help us in thinking about this question?

D Find out

Choose one or two of the subjects below and find out all you can about them. History books, geography books, biology books, religious education books and encyclopaedias may be useful. You could also use reference books in your school or public library to look up some of the names and places.

1 *The Second World War*
Find out about Pearl Harbor and how Japan entered the Second World War. What did General Orde Wingate and the Chindits do? How did the war with Japan end?

2 *The Far East*
Find out about the countries in the Far East today, including Japan, Burma, Thailand and Cambodia.

3 *Diseases*
Find out about the diseases mentioned in this story: beriberi, malaria, diphtheria, leprosy and dysentery. In each case, find out what the symptoms are and how people catch the disease. In which countries are the diseases still a serious problem? How are they treated?

4 *Buddhism*
Who was Gautama Buddha? How did Buddhism start? What is a Buddhist temple like? How do Buddhist monks live? What do Buddhists believe about suffering, reincarnation and the right way to live?

28

USEFUL INFORMATION

More books to read
Buddhism, by Trevor Ling (Ward Lock Educational) (P).
Miracle on the River Kwai, by Ernest Gordon (Fontana) (T).
The Naked Island, by Russell Braddon (Laurie) (T).
Prisoner of the Jungle: John Dodd, by Diana Norman (Lutterworth) (P).
Seventy Days to Singapore, by Stanley L. Falk (Hale) (T).
The Story of Changi, by David Nelson (L. Cooper) (T).
The Way of the Buddha, by Cottie Arthur Burland (Hulton Educational) (P).

(T) = suitable for teachers and older pupils
(P) = suitable for younger pupils

Film
The Singapore Story (30 min), black and white. Tells of the imprisonment of Bishop J. L. Wilson by the Japanese, following the fall of Singapore. Available from CTVC Film Library, Foundation House, Walton Road, Bushey, Watford WD2 2JS.

Filmstrip
Buddhism (colour, with script and comprehensive notes). Available from Educational Productions Ltd, Bradford Road, East Ardsley, Wakefield, West Yorkshire WF3 2JN.

29